WHAT IS STEAM?

THE TECHNOLOGY IN STEAM

BY THERESA EMMINIZER

Gareth Stevens
PUBLISHING

Please visit our website, www.garethstevens.com. For a free color catalog of all our high-quality books, call toll free 1-800-542-2595 or fax 1-877-542-2596.

Cataloging-in-Publication Data
Names: Emminizer, Theresa.
Title: The technology in STEAM / Theresa Emminizer.
Description: New York : Gareth Stevens Publishing, 2024. | Series: What is STEAM? | Includes glossary and index.
Identifiers: ISBN 9781538285565 (pbk.) | ISBN 9781538285572 (library bound) | ISBN 9781538285589 (ebook)
Subjects: LCSH: Technology–Juvenile literature.
Classification: LCC T48.E46 2023 | DDC 600–dc23

Published in 2024 by
Gareth Stevens Publishing
2544 Clinton Street
Buffalo, NY 14224

Designer: Leslie Taylor
Editor: Theresa Emminizer

Photo credits: Series Art (background art) N.Savranska/Shutterstock.com; Cover Chaay_Tee/ Shutterstock.com; p. 5 Monkey Business Images/Shutterstock.com; p. 7 George Rudy/ Shutterstock.com; p. 9 Ladanifer/Shutterstock.com; p. 11 pikselstock/Shutterstock.com; p. 13 Max kegfire/Shutterstock.com; p. 15 wutzkohphoto/Shutterstock.com; p. 17 bbernard/Shutterstock.com; p. 19 Prostock-studio/Shutterstock.com; p. 21 Chaay_Tee/Shutterstock.com.

Printed in the United States of America

Some of the images in this book illustrate individuals who are models. The depictions do not imply actual situations or events.

CPSIA compliance information: Batch #CSGS24: For further information contact Gareth Stevens at 1-800-542-2595.

Find us on

CONTENTS

Boldface words appear in the glossary.

What Is Technology?

Technology is using science, **engineering**, and other fields to invent, or make, useful tools and find the answers to problems. The word technology can also be used to talk about a device, or tool, that was **created** with technology.

Technology All Around

Whether or not you know it, you use technology every day. Car technology helps us get places quickly and safely. Phone and computer technology helps us **communicate** with each other. **Energy** technology powers our world. Technology is all around us!

In Our Bodies

Doctors use medical technology to save lives and help people be healthy. They use **robotics** to help them do **surgeries**. Pacemakers are technological devices used to help control a person's heartbeat. Prosthetics are artificial, or human-made, body parts.

At Home

Does your home have a dishwasher or washing machine? What about a refrigerator? Inventors designed, or made, these home technologies to help make people's lives easy. The **electricity** used to power these machines is a kind of technology too.

At School

Some technology helps us learn, find out facts, gain knowledge, and communicate with one another. This is called information technology. You likely use these devices—such as computers or tablets—at school or to do your homework.

To Communicate

Some information technology is also communication technology. Smart devices such as tablets and phones make it possible for you to talk to people across the world! Do you ever **video** call friends or loved ones? That's communication technology!

For Fun!

Do you have any electronic toys? Do you play video games? Do you watch TV? These things are different kinds of entertainment, or fun, technology! Virtual reality is a kind of entertainment technology people can use to pretend they're somewhere else.

Technology Skills

There are many different fields of technology. But all who study and create technology share a set of skills. They must be curious. They must think outside of the box to come up with new ways to answer questions.

Is Technology for You?

Do you like math and science? Are you interested in devices and how they work? Do you think about new ways to solve, or fix, problems or make life easier? If so, technology might be the path for you!

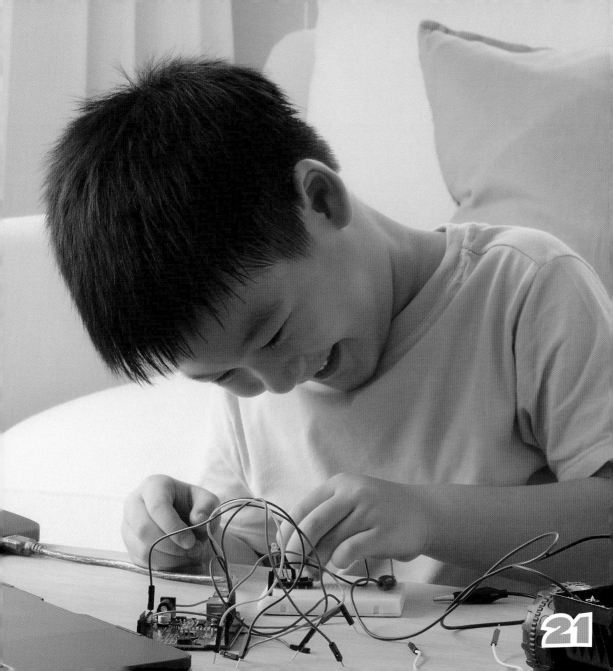

GLOSSARY

communicate: To share thoughts or feelings by sound, movement, or writing.

create: To make.

electricity: The flow of electrical power.

energy: Power used to do work.

engineering: The use of math and science to build better objects, or things.

robotics: Having to do with robots.

surgery: A medical treatment used for injuries and illnesses that involves operations.

video: Moving pictures that can be seen on a phone or computer screen.